AF483626

THE TRAVELER'S QUICK GUIDE
to TANTRIC YOGA

A sensual and spiritual journey through longing,
discipline, healing, and love.
He thought he was searching for the woman of his
dreams. In truth, he was being prepared to meet her.

BY LU & MATT

The Restless Mind

He first met her in the private theater of his own mind. Not as a face, not as a name, but as a feeling — a feminine presence that seemed to live just beyond the edge of thought. She came to him in moments of silence, between breaths, after long workouts, in the hush before sleep. He imagined a woman who was powerful yet soft, athletic yet graceful, beautiful yet deeply aware. Not only someone to desire, but someone to recognize.

He had spent years chasing achievement, discipline, and control. Yet beneath his ambition lived a deeper ache: the wish to be fully seen, fully chosen, fully joined. He wanted not just passion, but union. Not just chemistry, but destiny. And so his journey began not on an airplane or a mountain path, but in the unruly landscape of his own longing.

The Temple of the Gym

The gym was where he built the outer man.
Steel, sweat, repetition — every lift became a prayer in disguise. His body transformed through discipline, but so did his spirit. Beneath the mirrors and weights, he discovered something tantric without yet knowing the word for it: energy could be cultivated, directed, refined.
He learned that desire was not weakness. Desire was fuel.
Each movement taught him presence. Each drop of sweat reminded him that the body was not separate from the soul.
He trained not simply to look strong, but to become worthy of a great love — grounded, vital, awake.
And sometimes, between sets, he would imagine her again: a blonde woman with an athlete's elegance, fierce eyes, and a quiet magnetism. She did not seem like fantasy. She felt like prophecy.

The Therapist's Room

Strength alone could not open the heart.
So he entered another kind of training: the therapist's room. No mirrors. No trophies. No music loud enough to drown the truth. There, he spoke of loneliness, fear, perfectionism, and the strange sorrow of wanting love so deeply that it became a private wound.
He learned how often men are taught to pursue without understanding themselves. He learned that longing can become grasping, and that real love cannot be seized — only invited. He learned to soften his grip on fantasy and become curious about reality.
In those conversations, something in him unraveled. Old pain rose. Old shame loosened. He began to understand that the feminine he sought outside himself was also calling him inward — toward tenderness, emotional courage, and honesty.
He was no longer searching for a woman to complete him. He was becoming a man capable of meeting her fully.

Yoga and the Inner Flame

Yoga changed the rhythm of his life.
At first it was difficult. His body resisted stillness more than exertion. In the gym he conquered; in yoga he surrendered. But breath by breath, posture by posture, he discovered another dimension of strength — the strength to remain open.
Tantric practice taught him that masculine and feminine are not opponents, but currents. Presence and flow. Stillness and movement. Devotion and surrender. The body became not an instrument of conquest, but a vessel of awareness.
On his mat, he stopped chasing visions of love and started feeling it as a living force inside him. A warmth in the spine. A softness in the chest. A calm behind the eyes. He no longer asked, "Where is she?" but, "Who must I become when she arrives?"
The answer was simple: whole, patient, and true.

San Pedro

His first true journey took him to San Pedro.
The air itself felt different there — slower, salt-rich,
touched by memory. Streets glowed with coastal color. The
sea stretched wide and ancient, as though it had watched
countless people arrive carrying unspoken questions.
He walked alone for hours, letting the town enter him.
Cafés, rooftops, beach paths, strangers with knowing
smiles. In San Pedro, he felt the tenderness of being
unguarded in a new place. Travel stripped him down. There
were no routines to hide inside, no familiar masks to wear.
At sunset, he sat facing the water and felt the strange peace
that comes when searching begins to loosen into trust.
Maybe love did not live at the end of pursuit. Maybe it
arrived when body, spirit, and place finally harmonized.
For the first time, he could feel that she was not only ahead
of him. She was moving toward him too.

The Woman in the Distance

He began noticing her everywhere, though never fully. A flash of blonde hair in a marketplace. The silhouette of an athletic woman at sunrise by the sea. A laugh carried by wind. Not literally her, perhaps — but symbols of readiness, reflections of the love he was now prepared to meet.

He had once imagined beauty in narrow terms: flawless, radiant, idealized. But the deeper he went into tantric understanding, the more beauty became energetic. It was not simply in the curve of a body or the symmetry of a face. It was in aliveness. Grace. Receptivity. Fire balanced by peace.

He still dreamed of a woman who was luminous, disciplined, sensual, and strong. Yet now he also dreamed of conversation, of trust, of shared silence, of partnership that endured after the heat of first desire.

His dream woman was no longer just an image. She was becoming a soul.

Bali

Then came Bali.
If San Pedro had softened him, Bali opened him. Jungle air, temple smoke, flower offerings, scooters passing beneath banyan trees — everything felt intimate with spirit. The island seemed to whisper that desire itself could be sacred when held with reverence.
He practiced yoga in open-air studios where rain sang on leaves. He meditated beside pools lit by candles. He learned from teachers who spoke of devotion not as fantasy, but as daily alignment — breath, body, intention, touch, truth.
In Bali he felt deeply masculine, but not hard. Strong, but not closed. He understood that the tantric path was not about getting what one wants. It was about becoming available to a more exalted kind of love.
And on one quiet evening, beneath a violet sky, he felt the unmistakable sensation that his life was approaching its turning point.

The Meeting

He met her simply.
Not in spectacle. Not in thunder. Not in the dramatic perfection of fantasy. He met her in presence.
She stood with the effortless posture of an athlete and the soft confidence of a woman who knew herself. Blonde hair, light on her skin, clear intelligent eyes. She carried beauty without performing it. And when she looked at him, he felt not the shock of conquest, but the calm of recognition.
Their first conversation moved as if it had already begun elsewhere. They spoke of travel, discipline, healing, embodiment, longing, and why some people spend years circling the love they are destined to grow into. She was Russian, yes — but more than any category, she was fully herself: graceful, direct, sensual, perceptive.
He had envisioned meeting the girl of his dreams. Instead, he found a woman with her own dreams, her own depth, her own path.
The connection was deep, beyond expectation.

Tantric Union

Their bond grew not from urgency, but from attunement. They moved toward each other through breath, listening, laughter, touch, and honesty. Tantra became not an exotic performance, but a way of being present. To sit close. To look longer. To speak truth without armor. To let desire be warm rather than hungry.

They practiced together — yoga in the morning, slow walks in the afternoon, intimate conversations at night. They learned each other's rhythms, wounds, pleasures, and silences. Their sensuality deepened because it was rooted in trust. Their romance deepened because it was rooted in respect.

He had once imagined winning a soulmate. Now he understood the greater miracle: a soulmate is not won, but welcomed.

And in welcoming her, he found he was finally welcoming life itself.

Fulfillment

Love changed the geography of his inner world.

The man who had once searched frantically through thought, effort, and fantasy now rested in partnership. Not because longing had vanished, but because longing had matured into devotion. He no longer needed to perform strength. He lived it quietly. He no longer feared vulnerability. He practiced it daily.

With her, he discovered that emotional fulfillment was not soft in the weak sense — it required discipline, humility, and courage. Spiritual fulfillment was not escape — it was embodiment. To love another person fully was to remain awake inside one's own life.

Their bond was sensual, yes, but more than that, it was reverent. It held both passion and peace. Adventure and homecoming.

In loving her, he did not lose himself. He finally arrived.

The End.